The Georgia Open History Library has been made possible in part by a major grant from the National Endowment for the Humanities: Democracy demands wisdom. Any views, findings, conclusions, or recommendations expressed in this collection, do not necessarily represent those of the National Endowment for the Humanities.

NATIONAL
ENDOWMENT
FOR THE
HUMANITIES

# GEORGIA'S PLANTING PRELATE

By **HUBERT B. OWENS**
*Professor of Landscape Architecture*
*University of Georgia*

INCLUDING

## AN ADDRESS ON HORTICULTURE

AT MACON, GEORGIA, IN 1851

By THE RIGHT REVEREND STEPHEN ELLIOTT, JR.

ATHENS
UNIVERSITY OF GEORGIA PRESS
1945

COPYRIGHT 1945
UNIVERSITY OF GEORGIA PRESS

Reissue published in 2021

Most University Press titles are available from popular e-book vendors.

Printed digitally

ISBN 9780820359953 (Hardcover)
ISBN 9780820359960 (Paperback)
ISBN 9780820359977 (Ebook)

PRINTED IN THE UNITED STATES OF AMERICA

BY HIGGINS-MCARTHUR COMPANY, ATLANTA, GEORGIA

## Foreword to the Reissue

Ministers employ various strategies in their sermons. Some turn to the jeremiad, perhaps in a cynical belief that people change only when chastised or made to fear the consequences of their behavior. Others prefer to expound beatitudes. In his 1851 address to the Central Agricultural Society of Macon, Georgia, Episcopal Bishop Stephen Elliott interwove the two forms in a secular message on the state's rural prospects. First, he indicted Georgians for their general lack of attention to the finer points of agriculture and gardening: they had done little when given much. He then applied balm to the sore, spending the bulk of his speech on the state's great horticultural prospects owing to its varied terrain, rich soils, and temperate climate. If Georgians had yet to make a Garden of Eden from their surroundings, it was not from a lack of heavenly materials. They could still have peaches and flowers in place of milk and honey. But what did it mean that the Deep South lacked horticultural ornamentation, and how might the dearth be corrected?

University of Georgia landscape architect Hubert B. Owens, editor of the 1945 University of Georgia Press edition of the address, provides a concise and essential biographical sketch of Elliott in the pages of Georgia's Planting Prelate that follow, describing his intertwining careers as minister, educator, and horticulturalist. Elliott, Owens observes, was interested in growing all sorts of things: spirits, minds, and plants. This passion for cultivation in its multiple forms led him to a variety of work, as, for example, president of the Georgia Historical Society, senior bishop of the Episcopal Church of the Confederacy, and cofounder of the University of the South. For all his passion for growth and learning, Elliott firmly remained a patrician of his time and place, rooted in a South of plantations, commodity crops, and hierarchies of both class and race. He was at his core both a planting and a paternalist prelate.

Owens also notes the influence of Andrew Jackson Downing on Elliott, as indeed Downing was influential for every antebellum American horticulturalist and landscape designer. Downing's vision of beautiful greenswards, gardens, and rural architecture—a sort of English pastoralism for the New World—shaped movements as diverse as garden cemeteries like Boston's Mount Auburn and recreational grounds like New York's Central Park. Elliott would almost certainly have read and been influenced by such Downing publications as Treatise on the Theory and Practice of Landscape Gardening and Fruit and Fruit Trees of America (the latter cowritten with Downing's brother, Charles). Most influential was a magazine that Downing edited, The Horticulturalist and Journal of Rural Art and Rural Taste, which became something of an arbiter of landscape and garden taste in the South as well as the North in the late 1840s. Downing would be killed in a steamship explosion just months after Elliott's Macon speech, but when the reverend stood in front of Georgia planters, the New York horticulturalist was at the height of his fame and influence.[1]

If it contains echoes of Downing and northeastern taste making, Elliott's address should also be read as an agricultural reform tract, classic in its admixture of admonishment regarding careless cultivation and boosterism for Georgia's prospects. Although it may seem peculiar that Elliott—a minister and nurseryman—spoke to an agricultural society, the fusion of these interests was natural for the place and time. Agricultural reform, or "improvement," had originated in Europe, swept across the northern states, and by the 1830s began to make inroads in the South. The most vocal southern reformer was Virginia's Edmund Ruffin, who as editor of the Farmers' Register (1833–43) touted a range of improvement campaigns such as amending soils to improve fertility, regular crop rotation, more intensive livestock management, and a reduced dependence on tobacco and cotton in favor of agricultural diversification. Ruffin was hardly alone; a number of other prominent planters spoke for reform in their respective states, including Alabama's Noah Cloud and South Carolina's Henry William Ravenel.[2]

Elliott's Macon address plainly speaks to some core southern reform issues. For example, he chides Georgians for creating, or at least permitting, soil erosion, lamenting Middle Georgia's gullies that fissured the face of the red clay „into the rugged wrinkles of an early decrepitude" (44). Another minister and agriculturalist, John R. Cotting, had similarly indicted Georgia's farmers less than a decade earlier in the state's first thorough geological and soils survey.³ Reformers also spoke often and publicly of the need for agricultural diversification, and here Elliott's speech most thoroughly dovetails with the aims of improvement. Thus Elliott's extended discussion of the potential of southern fruit production anticipated and encouraged interest in such crops as peaches and experiments with citrus. (Perhaps the fullest demonstration of Elliott's vision came in the work of Louis and Prosper Berckmans, a father and son originally from Belgium who, beginning in the late 1850s, developed Augusta's Fruitland Nursery into a center of southern pomology.)⁴

Almost as important as agricultural diversification and sustained productivity were beauty and ornamentation, and Elliott epitomizes these aspects of improvement. Ornamental horticulture and landscape design may seem luxuries more than necessities for an agrarian people, but reformers imagined the cultivation and ornamentation of the countryside as two sides of the same coin. Planting flowers and fruit trees, constructing greenhouses, and laying out orchards were symbols of permanence. And antebellum southerner elites were at once a people on the move—always southwestward in pursuit of the main chance on a new cotton frontier—and deeply concerned about their transience. There was a fine line between a shifting culture and a shiftless one. To literally root oneself in a landscape through sustained efforts to beautify it was to project stability and order, for Elliott believed, "horticulture . . . is the science of a settled and permanent population, not the pursuit of a people struggling for bread and existence" (22). Elliott and his sympathizers were literally planting their history and future in Georgia soil alongside their peaches and camellias.

Elliott's speech might also be read as a defense of slavery, strange as this might seem at first blush. After all, the address itself contains not a single mention of "slave" or "slavery" (though Owens does rather uncritically repeat claims that Elliott was widely admired as a friend of the enslaved people). The reverend comes closest to the subject in his last point, when outlining the challenges horticulture faced in Georgia and the nature of planting, although in that passage it is the autonomous and authoritarian nature of planters that he sees as an obstacle, with no attention given to the human subjects of that authority. Elliott seems to have comfortably reconciled the plantation system and his faith. In a later address at the outbreak of the Civil War he simultaneously exalted the Episcopal Church's missionary work to enslaved people, praised their masters' paternalism, and instructed the state's clergy to cease their prayers for the president of the United States and in their place to pray for Jefferson Davis and the Confederacy.[5] Elliott's Macon speech swept the enslaved from the picture as neatly as he wished artful landscape architecture might hide the "appendages of necessity"—the „dirty negroes grinning at you from every door"—from the vistas of southern rural seats (43).

Yet Elliott's speech was also a defense of white Georgians' way of life, and to defend the South's planting scene was to defend its central economic institution. The commercial fruit orchards and beautified plantations of Elliott's vision were spaces he assumed would be built and tended by enslaved people. And the commodity crops that occupied the bulk of their toil, most notably cotton, produced the wealth that made horticultural experimentation, pleasure gardens, and greenswards possible. Although Elliott makes nods to the importance of horticulture for the state's smallholders, his message is directed almost exclusively to the planting class. Indeed, Owens notes that Elliott's own plans for his Montpelier Institute and its associated farm relied on enslaved laborers to reshape and beautify the property near Macon.[6] To build a permanent, beautiful plantation world would be the best evidence of all that slavery was not a morally or economically bankrupt system. Indeed, his kindred spirit Edmund Ruffin explicitly linked the success of the two, noting that enslaved labor could assist in improvement efforts such as amending fields. (In his Essay on Calcareous Manures [1832], Ruffin included an appendix that calculated the annual "cost of the labor" of enslaved men, women, and horses put to work spreading marl, a source of lime.) Agricultural improvement would in turn produce more food and support larger populations of slaves, reducing the practice of "the breeding and selling of slaves," which kept old plantations along the Atlantic seaboard afloat. Improvement would not end the system of slavery, as Ruffin framed it; it would instead provide a firm and (in his mind) more humane foundation in permanent agriculture.[7]

This, Elliot believed, would be the correct outcome. A beautiful and stable landscape in which white Georgians could enjoy the fruits of their labors (and of their enslaved laborers) without having to look to fresh land in the West was the most moral of all future worlds. Artful landscapes would reflect a righteous and rooted people. In this view nothing at all could be more practical than horticultural ornamentation, as the very future of the state rested on its practice. It was at once an expansive and a restricted vision, one soon to be unmade by the Civil War.

DREW SWANSON

## Notes

1. David Schuyler, *Apostle of Taste: Andrew Jackson Downing, 1815–1852* (Baltimore, Md.: Johns Hopkins University Press, 1996). On Downing and garden cemeteries, see Aaron Sachs, "American Arcadia: Mount Auburn Cemetery and the Nineteenth-Century Landscape Tradition," *Environmental History* 15, no. 2 (April 2010): 206–35. For Downing's role in inspiring the idea and design of Central Park, see Roy Rosenweig and Elizabeth Blackmar, *The Park and the People: A History of Central Park* (Ithaca, N.Y.: Cornell University Press, 1998), 29–30, 123–25.

2. Edmund Ruffin, *Nature's Management: Writings on Landscape and Reform, 1822–1859*, ed. Jack Temple Kirby (Athens: University of Georgia Press, 2000); Steven Stoll, *Larding the Lean Earth: Soil and Society in Nineteenth-Century America* (New York: Hill & Wang, 2002); Weymouth T. Jordan, "Noah B. Cloud's Activities on Behalf of Southern Agriculture," *Agricultural History* 25, no. 2 (April 1951): 53–58; Hayden R. Smith, *Carolina's Golden Fields: Inland Rice Cultivation in the South Carolina Lowcountry, 1670–1860* (Cambridge: Cambridge University Press, 2020), chap. 6.

3. John Ruggles Cotting, *An Essay on the Soils and Available Manures of the State of Georgia, with the Mode of Application and Management Founded on a Geological and Agricultural Survey* (Milledgeville, Ga.: Park & Rogers, 1843). On this survey's context, see Paul S. Sutter, *Let Us Now Praise Famous Gullies: Providence Canyon and the Soils of the South* (Athens: University of Georgia Press, 2015), 24–25.

4. The best recent study of the intersection of Georgia fruit culture and agricultural improvement is William Thomas Okie, *The Georgia Peach: Culture, Agriculture, and Environment in the American South* (Cambridge: Cambridge University Press, 2016).

5. Stephen Elliott, *Address of the Rt. Rev. Stephen Elliott, D. D., to the Thirty-Ninth Annual Convention of the Protestant Episcopal Church, in the Diocese of Georgia* (Savannah, Ga.: John M. Cooper and Company, 1861), 12, 16–17.

6. William M. Mathew, *Edmund Ruffin and the Crisis of Slavery in the Old South: The Failure of Agricultural Reform* (Athens: University of Georgia Press, 1988).

7. Edmund Ruffin, *An Essay on Calcareous Manures* (Petersburg, Va.: J. W. Campbell, 1832), 198, 228–233.

# GEORGIA'S PLANTING PRELATE

By HUBERT B. OWENS

RECORDED information concerning landscape gardening in Georgia and the lower South during the first half of the nineteenth century is rare. The same is true, to a lesser degree, with horticulture. It is the purpose of this booklet to bring to light a little known address dealing with these subjects, which was delivered before the Southern Central Agricultural Society in Macon, Georgia, in 1851.[1] This address gives a good picture of the horticultural and ornamental gardening situation in Georgia at that time. It also points out Georgia's opportunities and needs in the development of commercial horticulture, and reveals the unusual possibilities afforded by the climate for creating beautiful country seats and gardens. The address is especially interesting today because of the unprecedented activity in landscaping private and public grounds during the past few years, and in Victory Gardens since the beginning of World War II. It is not only interesting for these reasons, but also because of the man who wrote and delivered it.

Strange to relate, the author of this dissertation was neither a landscape gardener nor horticulturist by profession, nor was he a planter whose interests were wholly absorbed by the agricultural pursuits of the day. Instead, he was first of all a clergyman, and in addition, was an educator, a brilliant scholar of the arts and sciences, a writer, a widely known and much sought after orator, and today is

[1] See Notes, page 52.

regarded as one of the great Southern gentlemen of the ante-bellum period. The person to whom I refer is the Right Reverend Stephen Elliott, the first Bishop of the Episcopal Church in Georgia.

When one becomes acquainted with Stephen Elliott's background, education, and duties as first Episcopal Bishop of Georgia, it is not difficult to comprehend his profound interest in landscape gardening and horticulture. He was also interested in other fields of endeavor, all of which aimed at the general improvement of Georgia; but this treatise deals mainly with his convictions regarding horticulture and landscape gardening.

Stephen Elliott was born in Beaufort, South Carolina, August 31, 1806. His father, Stephen Elliott, was a widely known editor of two volumes on botany, founder and co-editor of *The Southern Review*, and a founder and president of the Bank of South Carolina. He also helped found the Medical College of South Carolina, and became its first professor of Botany and Natural History. In 1796 he married Esther Habersham, a member of one of Georgia's best known families. The future Bishop claimed the states of both of his parents as his own, and always evinced a deep interest in the affairs of Georgia and South Carolina.

Stephen was given a thorough education. In 1812 his parents moved to Charleston where he studied at a private school. At the age of sixteen he entered the sophomore class at Harvard University. The next year, because his father wanted him to complete his college training in his native state, Elliott transferred to South Carolina College and graduated in 1825 with third honors. He then studied law under Mr. James L. Petigrew, one of the foremost lawyers of the South, and helped in editing *The Southern Review*.

Stephen Elliott was admitted to the bar in 1827, and after practicing law in Charleston a few years, moved to Beaufort, South Carolina. The charm, refinement, and culture of this secluded coastal town appealed deeply to him and he came to love the people of the community. In the midst of a gay and successful life in Beaufort, he was caught up by the challenge of the new religious awakening sweeping the country, and it was here in 1832 that he made the decision to enter the ministry.

He was ordained a deacon three years later and after officiating for a brief period as minister in charge of the parish at Wilton, South Carolina, was elected chaplain and professor of Sacred Literature and Christian Evidences at South Carolina College. In this position he exerted a great influence on the student body, while his reputation for scholarship and eloquence became widespread. He was ordained a priest in 1836.

Elliott filled the post of professor and chaplain at this institution for five years. In 1840, at the age of thirty-three, he was elected first Bishop of Georgia and was consecrated Bishop at Christ Church, Savannah, on the 28th of February, 1841. To this new Diocese of Georgia he brought the prestige of his name and a missionary zeal.

The first several decades after the War of the Revolution was a rather barren period for the Episcopal Church in Georgia. This was due, in part, to the association in the minds of the public of the Episcopal Church with the Church of England, at a time when feeling was strong against Great Britain both because of the Revolutionary War and the War of 1812. Another contributing factor was that the Episcopal Church had no Bishop in Georgia at that time, and was loosely organized. When Stephen Elliott took over his duties as Bishop of Georgia there were only six active congregations in the State— Christ Church, Savannah; St. Paul's, Augusta; Christ Church, St. Simons Island; Christ Church, Macon; Trinity Church, Columbus; and Grace Church, Clarksville.

Within the next ten years Bishop Elliott established Episcopal Churches in the following places: Darien, Savannah, Milledgeville, Marietta, Glynn County, Effingham County, Athens, Rome, Etowah Valley, Atlanta, Talbotton, St. Marys, Augusta, Madison, and Montpelier. In addition to his regular visits to the churches in these places, he also made missionary trips to Lexington, Washington, the Ogeechee

River section, Albany, and other scattered points in the State. This was the period when "cotton was king" and the Georgia planters were prosperous, but the remarkable success in organizing and establishing the Episcopal Church in Georgia seems to have been due almost entirely to the inspired ability and personality of this one man.

It was natural that Elliott would be interested in education. Coming directly from his professorship at South Carolina College to Georgia in 1841, to find that the Baptists, Methodists, and Presbyterians had, in the 1830's, established colleges at Penfield, Covington, and Milledgeville, respectively, he doubtless felt it his duty to promote an institution of higher learning for Episcopalians. The first year he took over his duties as Bishop, he started the Georgia Episcopal Institute at Montpelier, located near Forsyth in Monroe County.

At the annual Convention of the Diocese in Macon in 1841, he reported, "The Christian liberality of G. B. Lamar, Esq., of Savannah, has enabled our Diocese to commence this work under the very best auspices. Having purchased the beautiful spot known as Montpelier Spring, he has presented it, with seven or eight hundred acres of land in its vicinity, to the Episcopal Church, vesting the property in a Board of Trustees, all of whom are members of our Church, the Bishop of the Diocese being, ex-officio, its President, with the injunction that the school shall be conducted upon Episcopal principles. The school has been organized by the election of the Rev. Charles Fey and his wife, late of Vermont, as its instructors, and of Samuel H. Fey, Esq., late of Savannah, as its Treasurer and Steward. Its growth must, at first, from its distinctive principles, be slow, but I trust that prudent management and strict discipline, and a religious spirit will win for it the support of the Christian Church."

In the beginning it was a school for both boys and girls, and in 1843 the Bishop engaged a graduate of Oxford University and a graduate of Leipzig University as teachers. It was his aim to provide the Diocese with the means for having their children educated according to Christian principles and the usual academic and classical attainments. Despite discouraging obstacles and financial difficulties, he persevered in this venture for several years. It was his plan to establish a stock farm to be cultivated by a slave force owned by the institution. The income from the farm should pay all the expenses of the school except the salaries of the professors, which would be charged against the amount received from tuition.

It became necessary for him to assume personal control of the Institute in 1845, for which purpose he removed his residence from Savannah to Montpelier. Due to the difficulty in finding a suitable headmaster, the boys' school was abandoned. In December, 1852, he resigned his position at Montpelier, as he felt the school no longer needed his presence. He secured an experienced lady, Miss M. M. Buell, to take charge of the Institute, and he returned to Savannah to assume the rectorship of Christ Church, along with his duties as Bishop.

It was during his residence at Montpelier that he was invited to address the Southern Central Agricultural Society at the annual Fair in Macon, October 29, 1851. The fact that he was chosen to speak on the subject of horticulture is evidence that he was regarded as an authority in this field, all of which is amply substantiated by the content of his address. Although he was not a "professional," apparently he was better informed on horticulture and the art of gardening in general than any other person living in Georgia.

His duties as Bishop carried him to all parts of the state, for in 1844 Bishop Elliott traveled six thousand miles. This gave him the opportunity to meet the leading planters and to observe and discuss with them their accomplishments in all fields of agriculture. On occasions, between 1841 and the time he presented this scholarly lecture at Macon, his duties carried him to points outside of Georgia. On one such trip to New York in 1841, he visited schools at Flushing so as to enable him to manage the Institute at Montpelier more intelligently. June 15th, this same year, he preached before the Board of Missions at St. James Church, Philadelphia. At various times after 1843 he visited Florida (which had no Bishop of its own until 1851) where he ministered to the parishes of Tallahassee, Monticello, Quincy, and Apachicola. In his report to the 29th Annual Convention of the Diocese, held at Trinity Church, Columbus, in May 1851, he tells of a meeting of the Council of Bishops which he attended in Cincinnati on October 1, 1850. Such trips to other sections of the country gave him the opportunity to become acquainted with the state of horticulture and landscape gardening in these places, and provided a basis for comparative statements made in his address.

The Bishop's speech shows that he read the current agricultural periodicals of the day and that he was well acquainted with the writings of Andrew J. Downing of Newburgh, New York, the leading authority on landscape gardening and horticulture in the United States between 1841 and 1851. Downing, who is regarded as the father of landscape architecture in America, wrote a number of books which dealt with the art of landscape gardening, rural architecture, etc., and edited a magazine entitled *The Horticulturist*, during the first decade of Elliott's bishopric. Downing's most famous book, *A Treatise on Landscape Gardening*, was published in 1841. This book carried the imposing sub-title, " . . . Adapted to North America; with a view to the improvement of country residences, comprising historical notices and general principles of the art, directions for laying out grounds and arranging plantations, the description and cultivation of hardy trees, decorative accompaniments of the house and grounds, the formation of pieces of artificial water, flower gardens, etc., with remarks on rural architecture." It was the first book by an American written on this subject, and it attained instant popularity both here and abroad. This book and all of Downing's works were widely read in the South, as well as other parts of the country, and the Bishop's address indicates that he was strongly influenced by Downing's writings.

The references to Montpelier in his speech reveal that Elliott also put into practice his own ideas regarding agriculture, floriculture, pomology, gardening, and architecture. Due to financial difficulties, the church discontinued its management of Montpelier Institute, and it went into private hands a few years after Bishop Elliott delivered his address at the Fair in Macon. Although little remains today to suggest the original layout, it must have been a delightful place in its time.[2] White's *Historical Collections of Georgia*, published in 1849, contains the following account of the Institute:

"The Episcopal Church is chiefly indebted to the liberality of G. B. Lamar, Esq., formerly of the city of Savannah, for this invaluable seminary.

"This school is located in Monroe county, about seventeen miles from Macon, fourteen from Forsyth, and six from the Macon and Western Railroad. Its advantages are not surpassed by those of any school in the United States. Until the property was purchased by Mr. Lamar, it was a favourite resort for invalids, who were attracted by its medicinal springs, healthful climate, and delightful temperature. Its natural beauties, which are rarely equalled, have been improved with the finest taste. The visitor needs only to see its extensive lawn, majestic groves, shady walks, beautiful gardens, and spacious buildings, to be in love with the spot. In addition to this, it is the permanent residence of the bishop of the diocese, a gentleman long distinguished for devoted piety and extensive literary attainments. His large and well selected library affords an inexhaustible source of entertainment and knowledge to the pupils. The course of instruction is thorough and complete; embracing every item that can contribute to fit a lady for the first stations in society. Its teachers are persons of high character and first rate abilities. They have been procured at great expense in Europe and America. It may be truly said that in this school true religion, useful learning, and polished refinement are inseparably united. The number of pupils varies from sixty to ninety. The applicants have generally been more than could be accommodated."

In the *Transactions of the Southern Central Agricultural Society*, published in 1852, are detailed lists of premium winners at the State

Fair staged by this organization in Macon in 1851. These lists show that people from all parts of Georgia entered exhibits in the following classes: Agricultural Products; Domestic Manufactures; Machinery; Livestock; Poultry; Furniture; Silk Manufactures; Horticulture; Floriculture; Painting; Printing, Drawing and Drafting; Needle, Shell and Wax Work; and Household Department. This publication includes a copy of Bishop Elliott's address delivered at the Fair and discloses the fact that he also entered exhibits. The judges on Horticulture awarded him a silver cup for the best and greatest variety of vegetables raised by one individual. Following is a report of the judges on Floriculture:

"The Committee on Floriculture beg leave to offer the following Report:

"That the limited time allowed for the inspection of the rare and beautiful specimens of green-house plants exhibited, did not permit so entire an examination as their merits deserved; and where all presented such high claims to meritorious mention, they can only select a few for particular notice. In the professional list, they cannot forbear to particularize Eriobotrina Japonica, Crinum Amabile, Torenia Asiatica, Melocactus Communis, Araucaria Brasilensis, from the collection of Bishop Elliott, at Montpelier, as excellent, and some magnificent specimens of their respective genera. They accordingly award—

IN THE PROFESSIONAL LIST

Rt. Rev. Bishop Elliott, of Montpelier, for the greatest variety and quantity of flowers, a Silver Cup worth $5.00.

Robert Nelson,[3] for the greatest variety and quantity of Dahlias, a premium of $2.00.

Robert Nelson, for the greatest variety and quantity of Roses, a premium of $2.00."

Bishop Elliott's display of vegetables is included on the non-professional list, but the committee of judges on Floriculture classed him as a professional. This was doubtless due to the facilities of the Montpelier Institute at his disposal for growing green-house plants, shrubs, roses, flowers, etc., and also the services of two gardeners, Mr. Patrick Fleming and Mr. Carolan.

A few years after leaving Montpelier, Bishop Elliott became identified with another educational enterprise. He, together with Bishop James Hervey Otey, of Tennessee, and Bishop Leonidas Polk, of Louisiana, founded the University of the South at Sewanee, Tennessee, the cornerstone of which was laid October 10, 1860. Moultrie Guerry in *Men Who Made Sewanee* says:

"Bishop Polk's devoted friend and idol was Stephen Elliott. 'Twin brothers,' they were called because of their age, congeniality, and partnership in founding the University of the South. In Elliott, Polk saw the cultural ideal for the University: he was a scholar in things scientific and literary, and a thinker ahead of his day. Polk eagerly enlisted Elliott's influence, which was great indeed both within and without the Church, and his matchless pen, which was eloquent in the cause of education and which has left its tracing in the early documents of the Founders."

Elliott was particularly helpful in serving as a commissioner of endowment and in choosing a suitable location for the University on the Cumberland plateau in Tennessee. Here, again, we find evidence of his convictions on landscape gardening, for, in addition to his helping choose a beautiful site for the University, he was largely responsible for securing a landscape plan to be used for the location of buildings and in developing the grounds of the campus.

For this purpose, Bishop John Henry Hopkins, of Vermont, a close personal friend of Elliott's, adept at landscape gardening, was chosen. His abilities even exceeded those of the Georgia Bishop in this particular field. Because of early training in drawing, painting, and engineering, he was able to draw professional plans. George R. Fairbanks, in his *History of the University of the South* says:

"Bishop Hopkins, of Vermont, among his other extraordinary and multiform accomplishments was distinguished for his architectural skill and refined taste in landscape gardening."

He was invited to come to Sewanee and prepare a plan for the campus. His great regard for Bishop Elliott and Bishop Polk, his sympathy with the great work they were undertaking, and his desire to earn some money to further an educational project in his own diocese, led him to accept the invitation. He spent three happy but laborious months there during the winter of 1859-1860, during which time he made a careful study of the topography and general features of the ground, "having the advantage of being on the mountain after the leaves had fallen, so that the general lay of the land could be more readily observed." At Christmas time that year, Bishop Elliott made a trip to Sewanee to confer with Hopkins.

An account of Bishop Hopkins' stay at Sewanee written by one of his sons states that Bishop Hopkins was impressed with finding sixty natural springs on the property and that "he was in raptures, too, with the place in other respects. All along the outskirts of the elevated plateau he found beautiful views of the valley and distant mountains; while the interior was filled with noble trees, the oak, hickory, walnut, chestnut, tulip tree, etc., and would constitute, when properly improved, the finest park one could desire. 'If Lake Champlain could be thrown in,' Bishop Hopkins remarked, 'it would be absolute perfection.'" During his three months' sojourn, Bishop Hopkins prepared maps of roads and avenues, plans for buildings, chose sites for buildings, and made several water-color sketches of striking views of Sewanee. Several of these drawings and sketches were destroyed at the time of the War Between the States.

Stephen Elliott was the senior Bishop of the Episcopal Church in the South during the War Between the States. His friendship with Bishop Hopkins, who was the presiding Bishop of the Church in the entire United States, and his moderation and good sense were great assets toward the amicable union of the churches North and South, which was consummated soon after hostilities ceased.

On December 21, 1866, Bishop Elliott died suddenly at his home in Savannah. His last sermon was preached the day before at Montpelier, the scene of his hopes and endeavors. He was only sixty-one years old, but had served as Bishop of Georgia for more than twenty-five years.

A few years before his death Bishop Elliott had been asked to consecrate an Episcopal church for colored people in Savannah named St. Stephen's, not for the first Christian martyr, as he supposed, but for himself. He was the St. Stephen this colored congregation knew and loved first hand. They looked up to him as their finest, wisest and noblest friend. In a memoir of the late Bishop written by Thomas A. Hanckel in 1867, a few months after Elliott's death, is the following account:

"At his burial they gave a touching and beautiful evidence of the love and reverence they bore him. The colored vestry of St. Stephen's asked to have the honor of carrying him to the grave; and it was granted to them. It did honor to them and to their Bishop. Considering the peculiar and momentous issues of the time, we think it was the grandest and most instructive spectacle, amidst all the solemn, mournful and agitating ceremonies of the day, on which the city of Savannah was hushed to listen to the footfalls of those who thus bore their Bishop to the tomb."

Edgar Legare Pennington, in an article written for the *Historical Magazine of the Protestant Episcopal Church,* states:

"He was a man of broad and varied interests: a preacher whose gifts were recognized throughout the Episcopal communion, a founder of institutions of higher learning, the president of the Georgia Historical Society. Bishop Elliott was one of the most prominent advocates of the right of the negro to enlightenment and justice; and he showed how a southern bishop, of patrician ancestry, dealt with the problem of slavery; his example suggests that when the cataclysm occurred, the slavery issue may well have been on its way to a peaceful solution.

"In a study of Stephen Elliott, we are able to trace the evolution of the culture of the newer South. Around him clustered movements which gradually moulded a frontier state into a settled one. The Georgia which he first knew was largely the Georgia of the old communities—Savannah, Augusta, and the towns along the Atlantic seaboard; during his lifetime the other sections were rapidly filled by white settlers from another stock, who replaced the red man, and who were at work developing new plantations and industries and laying foundations for a populous section."

# ADDRESS ON HORTICULTURE

*Delivered before the Central Agricultural Society of Georgia at Macon, October 29, 1851*

By RT. REV. STEPHEN ELLIOTT, JR.

IT SEEMS, at first sight, very astonishing that, in a State, so richly blessed as Georgia with all the advantages of nature, so little attention should have been paid to Horticulture, either as a science or an art. Whether we grope our way through the tangled luxuriance of our Eastern shores, or climb the rugged steeps of our northern mountains, or saunter over the gently rounded hills of our midland counties, the eye of taste perceives around it, in rich abundance, the rarest elements of all the arts which make up this fascinating pursuit. Each portion of the State has its peculiar beauties, and it is not easy to decide their relative claims to admiration and enjoyment. While the level counties of our seaboard lack the line of beauty which belongs to the swelling slopes of our hill country, and are deficient in the ever changing hues which play around the mountain tops and light up as with fire the foliage of their gorges; they yet stand unrivaled in the magnificence of their outspread forests, in their overarching masses of foliage and flowers, in their broad sheets of water, rippling up in pellucid brightness to the very feet of the beholder, and above all, in the capabilities which a climate almost devoid of frost affords to the intermixture of tropical luxuries with those which belong to our peculiar zone. Or if our rolling midland counties are denied the venerable glories of gigantic and moss crowned trees, and cannot boast such rank luxuriance of vegetation, and are doomed to roll down forever to the ocean, rivers "yellow as the Tiber," they yet have their own arrangement of hill and valley, of rock and glen, of sighing waterfalls and grassy knolls which work out for them the invariable compensations of nature. And if again, we change the scene and transport ourselves to the mountain region of the State, we often feel, as we gaze out upon those boundless views, which Claude would have delighted to paint, or watch the sunsets as they change from gold to purple, and from purple to blue, and from blue to the dull gray of an indistinct twilight, or look shudderingly into the chasms through which the agitated waters are struggling to force their way, that association must at last decide among their various charms, and that the claims of nature, in each particular section, must be assisted by the recollections of childhood and the fancies of our dreamy youth, ere it can gain the triumph over its rival scenes. All, all are beautiful, and crowned as is this natural glory by a soil rich as the most ardent worshiper of nature could desire, and a climate fit for almost every culture, and a profusion of materials for all artificial appliances, it is, indeed, as we observed just now, at first sight, a source of wonder and reproach that we should be so very far behind less favored countries in every branch of Horticulture, from the vegetable that speaks to our absolute necessities to the exotic flower which ministers only to our luxuries.

But it is only at first sight and to the superficial observer, that there is any real ground either for wonder or reproach. The reasons of our backwardness lie upon the very surface and are as good excuses as people generally offer for their faults. In adducing them, we mean them merely as excuses, without pretending to maintain that we have not been somewhat to blame or that we ought not immediately to set about the correction of our errors; and as they lead us very naturally into the midst of the subject which I have been appointed to treat, I shall dwell upon them at greater length than they would deserve, considered simply as excuses. The knowledge of the difficulties which stand in the way of our improvement is the first step towards their removal, and is the surest pledge of our intention to be wiser and better for the future.

The greatest, and I fear the most incurable difficulty, in the way of our advancement in Horticulture, arises out of the very kindness and profusion of nature herself. She has showered her richest gifts so lavishly upon us, that we have grown accustomed, like all spoiled and pampered children, to demand and receive every thing at her hands, and to become mere dependent idlers upon her bounty. We see around us a Flora, springing up spontaneously at our feet, so rich in variety, so exquisite in beauty, so delicious in perfume, that we can scarce believe that art can add any thing to our resources. We listen complacently to the admiration which strangers lavish upon the grace of our woods, the sweetness of our flowers, the flavor of our fruits, the genial breath of our atmosphere and are satisfied to enjoy them in their wild and untrained excellence. And should we take the trouble of introducing any thing rare or beautiful into our gardens, we are fain to treat it as we have been wont to treat our indigenous productions and leave it to the unassisted kindness of nature. Because we have so many good things without any trouble, we are unwilling to take any pains to have them better, and the strong temptation lies heavy upon the people of an indolent climate, to be content with good things which cost no pains, rather than be troubled about supreme excellence in any thing.

Another obstacle to our progress in Horticulture has arisen from the recent settlement of much of our State, and from the necessity which has been laid upon our people of hewing out for themselves homes in the forest and the wilderness. Because Georgia was reckoned among the old thirteen States, and because of her rapid strides, of late years, in physical improvement people find it difficult to realize that the largest and most valuable portion of the State has been settled within the last thirty and much of it within the last fifteen years.[5] The very spot on which I now stand, surrounded by this large assemblage of intelligent and elegant people, encompassed with the rich offerings of science and of art, was but yesterday the home of the Indian. Georgia has been in the condition of an unfortunate stripling, who has shot up beyond his years and from whom is expected a maturity of wisdom, of manners, of conduct, correspondent with his maturity of physical development. Look only at his growth and you would be warranted in demanding that he should think as a man, that he should speak as a man, that he should act as a man: but ask the youth his age, and you will no longer be surprised that he has not altogether "put away childish things." And so with our own fair Georgia. Was she really as old, as appearances in many things would warrant us in supposing her, we might ask for her country seats, for her parks, for her gardens, for her orchards, and be disappointed if we did not find them worthy of such a soil and such a climate. But when we reflect that emigrants to Alabama and Mississippi and Louisiana, passed over a Federal Road[6] through Indian tribes to reach those States, and were protected in those journeys within the State of Georgia by United States agencies and United States soldiery—that within the recollection of our children, the war whoop was heard upon our Western limits, we should be unreasonable to expect such luxurious appliances as surround the homes of Massachusetts or New York, or Pennsylvania. As well might we have asked for these things in those States a century ago, as demand them now at our hands. And most assuredly if you had made the demand of them you would have received the very reply which we now make: "We have been too busy in clearing our forests, in sheltering our heads, in providing for our actual necessities to have any time for extraneous pursuits." Horticulture, except in its lowest branches, is the science of a settled and permanent population, not the pursuit of a people struggling for bread and existence. And already do we perceive, in the various societies which exist within the State; in the important part which Horticulture is playing in this very fair; in the corner which is allowed it in all our agricultural papers; and above all, in the deep interest which individuals are taking in it all over our land, the evidence that a more settled and permanent population will rapidly wipe away our reproach from among men.

A third difficulty which has stood in the way of our improvement in Horticulture has been owing to the great difference which exists between our soil and climate, and those whence has been drawn all our book knowledge of this pursuit. A climate peculiarly wet, an atmosphere remarkably humid, a soil needing drainage at every point, has furnished for us, whose climate, atmosphere and soil are the very antipodes of those of England, the theory and practice of Horticulture. The English treatises and the English practice may do well enough for the Northern States, although in many particulars unsuitable to them; but for us they are not only useless but absolutely pernicious. The general principles of the science are the same, of course, every where; but the practical application has to be worked out for each peculiar climate. In this way, we at the South, have had every thing to do for ourselves; and deriving almost our whole literature from England and the North, we have been perplexed with numberless theories, and rules having no application among ourselves.[7] The countries whence we should have derived our horticultural maxims, Italy, Spain, and the countries bordering the Levant, have, in great measure been locked against us, and we have floundered on, through what should have been a most sad experience, had not nature been really so kind as to do for us, in spite of our mistakes, what we never should have been able to do for ourselves. And hitherto, most of the experience which has been wrought out through the laborious exertion and observation of individuals has died with them, or has lain dormant with those who have gained it, for lack of societies and journals through which to compare it with the experience of others, or communicate it to beginners.[8] The consequence has been that each individual, or each generation, as the case might be, has been obliged to go over the same ground as its predecessor—to commit the like errors, to incur the like useless expense, to waste almost a life-time in acquiring knowledge and gaining positions which a few weeks reading or a few hours conversation with one who had been over the ground, might have given him. We have not been permitted to stand upon the shoulders of a previous generation. We have been forced to be pioneers in every thing connected with Southern Horticulture. Why, even to this day, we have not a decent work upon the very commonest topics of vegetable or floral cultivation adapted to the South. It has been impossible, therefore, for any progress to have been made, save as neighbor might communicate to neighbor the results of his experience, or parent might hand down to child, traditional rules of action and modes of operation.

Moreover, there has been at the South no pecuniary stimulus to urge on the improvement of Horticulture. In England and the Northern States, most of the great Horticulturists have been the owners of large establishments for the propagation and sale of vegetables, fruits and flowers. The proximity of large cities, the concentration of wealth, and the inevitable growth of luxury have enabled these Horticulturists to spare neither labor nor expense in procuring, propagating and circulating plants of whatever kind, and thus filling, at a small expense, the gardens, orchards and greenhouses of their fellow-citizens. It is from these depositories that the great mass of the flowers and fruits and vegetables, which illustrate the English and Northern exhibitions is obtained; and while there are really many more private collections at the South, we cannot concentrate these things, because they have been reared merely for individual pleasure and not for profit or show. Until very lately, with the exception of the Noisette garden near Charleston, I know of no Horticultural establishment among ourselves, that was not a mere branch of some Northern house.[9] And this—not because fruits and flowers were not valued; not because there was not a constant importation going on of these things from the North—but simply because it was considered mean to sell any thing except cotton, rice, tobacco, wheat, or some other of the great staples of the country. Every body had flowers and fruits, such as they were, and he was quite ready to give his neighbor all that he had: to sell them to him would have been considered quite beneath the dignity of a farmer or planter. Horticulture has suffered, like every other branch of art at the South, from the absorbing pursuit and immense profit arising out of the cultivation of the leading staples of the country.

The last, though by no means the least reason which I shall offer for the backwardness of Horticulture among us, has sprung out of that which ought to have been its chief support. We are universally a planting people, and planters are the least gregarious people upon the face of the earth. Living separate and apart, each upon his own estate, the planter is an independent power: he is Lord of all he surveys, and he frames his own conduct upon the basis of this individual sovereignty. The social tie—the current of fashion—the compromise of opinion is but little known to him. He thinks for himself, he speaks for himself, he acts for himself; and unless a movement, of whatever kind or for whatever purpose, commends itself to his individual judgment, he is but little swayed by the opinions or desires of others. It is very difficult to move such a being out of the routine of old practices and traditional modes of action, especially as he has a profound contempt for "novelties that disturb his peace" or for book farming of any kind. His father grew rich upon such and such an experience, and it would be filial irreverence for him to engage in any new fangled schemes for the improvement of his homestead or his grounds. Such men it is not easy to collect into societies—the instrumentality of the present day for the advancement of every science and art. Even now, we find it exceedingly difficult in an agricultural State to maintain agricultural societies promising profit and recompense to the members: how much more difficult to originate and carry on Horticultural societies which seem much more connected with mere ornament and luxury.

Such are the reasons which, in my opinion, have placed and kept us in the horticultural condition in which we find ourselves today. I trust that the time has come when many of these obstacles will be removed out of the way. Our population is rapidly becoming more permanent; our planters are beginning to abandon the policy of running after new land and are entering upon plans of improvement for their homes. The growth of our towns is also furnishing a nucleus around which horticultural societies will be formed and create a taste for things now neglected and perchance despised. The various journals in which horticulture is associated with agriculture, will create a literature of flowers that will soon produce the books which are wanted for direction and guidance, and as nursery gardens are beginning to be formed, we shall soon see, I trust, the stimulus of profit swelling the rising tide of horticulture. How to overcome the profusion of nature, I really know not; and it is almost as difficult a problem how to arouse a horticultural zeal among our rural population. But patience and perseverance will overcome even these, and when overcome, they will prove the most powerful means of urging forward the delightful pursuit which we are now considering.

The most fascinating, at the same time that it is the most ornamental branch of horticulture, is that which stands connected with the flower garden and the green-house. I take no notice, in my remarks, of the hot-house, for in the larger part of our State, we do not require, except perhaps for a night or two during the depth of winter, any greater heat than can be maintained in a well built green-house, managed with skill and judgment. This I know from experience. For several years, I have used one, not by any means well guarded, and have found artificial heat necessary only for one or two nights in each winter, even when I was cultivating very delicate plants belonging to the tropical climate of the East and West. In this department of horticulture, we are, perhaps, taking the State as a whole, better advanced than in any other branch of this art. And this has arisen, partly from the felicity of our climate and partly from their having been the peculiar province of the ladies—the heralds of all refinement and all elegance. If horticulture consisted merely in the plenty and variety of beautiful flowers that could be collected with ease at any given point; if it did not include as well the arrangement and cultivation of those flowers, the carrying them by artificial means to their highest perfection, the production of new varieties by hybridization, the constant enlargement of our flora by importation and acclimation, I should not admit that we were at all behind any part of the Union in this branch of the art. The genial kindness of our climate assimilates the most precious plants of other countries to itself, and exotics like the Camellia, the Oleander, the Gardenia, the Tea Roses, are rapidly becoming indigenous in the milder portions of our State.[10] When these beautiful genera were first introduced among us, they were treated in Carolina and Georgia as they are treated in England and the Northern States, nursed and protected into feebleness and ugliness. By degrees we learned that our climate and soil were peculiarly well adapted to them, and now the Gardenias and the Tea Roses are as much at home in all lower and middle Georgia as in any portion of the world, and the Oleander and Camellias are rapidly becoming weeds in the Eastern counties of the State. In many of the gardens in Savannah, and especially in the grounds of the late Mr. LeConte,[11] of Liberty County, there are seasons of the year when one literally walks upon Camellias, and their seed is freely matured in the open air. Exotics like these, rifled from Africa, Persia, China, when added to our native Flora, furnish us, at very little expense, a profusion of exquisite flowers, and there is scarcely a section of the State in which, at certain seasons, bouquets might not be furnished, that it would puzzle Mr. Paxton, with all the riches of Chatsworth at his command, to rival or surpass.[12] Even in our mountain region, the bleakest and most sterile portion of our State, the Kalmias, the Rhododendrons, the Azaleas, the Robinias, give a richness and glory to the rocky carpet over which they are spread, that might enable it to compete with the gayest patterns that leave the looms of Flanders or Persia. We have no lack of flowers, of beautiful flowers, but we have great lack of skill in the cultivation of them, and still greater lack of taste in the arrangement of them about our houses; and we are doing literally nothing in the production of new varieties. We take our flowers very much as we take every thing else from the North and from Europe, just as they please to give them to us, and take no pains to originate new varieties and so bring them into tribute to us. We are exhibiting the wonderful anomaly of a fertile soil, a felicitous climate, an atmosphere assimilating to itself almost every plant subjected to its influence, made tributary, from lack of enterprise and industry, to countries possessing none of these advantages, and struggling for six months of the year against ice and frost and snow. Why should this be so? Why should we not turn the current of trade in flowers as we are rapidly turning it by our steam boats, in vegetables and fruits? We can place vegetables upon the northern tables perfectly matured, before their climate will permit them to be even planted, and if we chose, we might supply, in like manner, the belles of New York and Philadelphia, with the richest ornaments of their boudoirs and drawing rooms. If you could witness the surprise of the northern invalids who resort to Savannah and the Eastern shores of Georgia and Florida, at the profusion of exquisite flowers that are poured in upon them, in mid-winter, from the gardens of its citizens, you would appreciate the advantage which we possess in climate and soil. And yet, despite all this, we are mere amateurs in Floriculture, and with the exception of the Noisette and Herbemont Roses, I really do not know one single contribution that we have made to the floral riches of the world through any exercise of art.[13] We are acting like a man of genius, who, with very little labor, can achieve as much as his rivals with all their pains, and yet is content to be only as learned and wise as they are, when God intended him to soar a higher flight and become one of the master spirits of the time. Because we can, through the blessing of nature, reach with ease an excellence like that of less favored countries, should we be satisfied with that? Should we, who are intended to be the foremost horticulturists of the world, permit others with every thing against them, to usurp our position and thrust us from our thrones? Away with such groveling views! Let us, in horticulture, as in every thing else, learn a nobler ambition, and make our land what God and nature intended it should be, a land of surpassing beauty and exceeding joys.

It is impossible, in an address like this, to enter into details—a few passing hints are all that I may introduce, and my friends must look for any thing more in the Soil of the South, where I trust we may often meet for mutual instruction and improvement. I would therefore merely state, that in preparing a flower garden, the point of importance is to secure a strong, permanent soil, rather than an over rich and over manured one. The naturally good soil of our State, deeply spaded and intermingled with the top soil of old fields and vegetable manure from the woods, makes the very best substratum for almost all flowers and shrubs. With this compost may be judiciously mingled some well rotted stable manure, say one fourth in quantity; and with clay soils some white sand; and with sandy soils some clay or pond earth. Upon such a compost as this, with a depth of eighteen inches, I have a Cloth of Gold rose which covered, in two years, the greater part of the front of a house, and climbed over the eaves, twenty-five feet from the ground, upon the roof; a La Marck, whose stem was in three years the size of a man's wrist; Banksias, Ophirie, Bignonias, Wistarias, all intermingling over the sides and roof of the house and crying out for room; and in the same soil the Amaryllis, the Lilium, the Gladiolus have all acquired a relative luxuriance and ask nothing but the most ordinary care. A strong and deep soil is what flowers need, and not an over manured one. The plants, in the latter soil, will be like children fed upon sweetmeats and confectionary, sickly, dyspeptic, always ailing. Those upon the strong, deep soil, like the rosy cheeked cherubs that have developed their muscles and painted their faces under the influence of wholesome natural diet and the pure air and bright skies of Heaven. Particular families of plants need special soils, and where it is desirable to cultivate these to perfection, recourse must be had to such mixtures as the books indicate, with this point, however, kept always in mind, that no books upon horticulture which we possess, are adapted to our climate. Their general directions must always be modified by such particular experience as can be gleaned from our own journals and amateurs of the State.

The green-house is generally considered a very expensive appurtenance to an establishment. This depends very much, of course, upon the size and style of the building. Like everything else, they can be made luxuries, and then they will be expensive, but in the South they are not necessarily so. In Europe and in the cities of the Northern States, where land is worth its area in gold, any structure is expensive; but with us space is abundant even in our towns, and the mere site of a building enters not into the calculation of its cost. Material, too, for building is abundant and cheap, and almost every planter has his own mechanics, who, with some instruction, could arrange a very neat structure of this sort. The only expense, therefore, to a planter, in money, would be the cost of the sash work and the glass, both of which have been very much reduced by the application of improved machinery. But in our mild climate there is a very excellent substitute for a greenhouse, requiring no expenditure exceeding five or ten dollars. This substitute is a pit dug in the earth to the depth of five or six feet, of any size the party may desire, and furnished with benches rising one above the other like the staging of a theater. Around the upper edge of this pit, run a wooden framework of a foot in height in front and two feet in the rear, with its sides sloping from rear to front, cover the top with frames attached by hinges to the rear, and instead of glass, enclose these frames with the common ten cent homespun of our factories, well saturated and tacked tightly as they can be drawn over the sides and ends of the frame. Such a pit as this will answer all the practical purposes of a green-house, and will give you through the winter, a succession of exotic flowers, and through the summer will deck your gardens with the riches of the East, as they continue to flourish in their sunk and concealed pots.

The fruit culture of Georgia is in a very anomalous condition. The remarks which I made respecting floriculture apply in some measure, although not so widely to Pomology. We have a great deal of very fine fruit scattered through the State, fine in appearance, fine in size, and above all fine in flavor, but we have no system, very little art, and above all no nomenclature. A delicious peach is handed us, whose skin peels off like that of a well boiled potato, the rich juice the while streaming down our fingers, and while the flesh melts in our mouth and the combined qualities of smell and taste and sight are gratified to the utmost, *'tis still only a peach,* and great astonishment is expressed at a desire to know any thing more about it. A dish of strawberries is placed upon the table—strawberries such as Peabody[14] only can raise—and while every one admires the size and flavor and delicacy, they are still only strawberries, and no body cares whether they are Hovey's, or Burr's, or Ross' or any body's else, who may have taken infinite pains in establishing a fine variety. And thus it happens that while we have good fruit of certain sorts, it is because we cannot help ourselves. It is thrust upon us by nature, and neglect it as we may, it still, under the favorable auspices of our climate and soil, is tolerably good, teaching us what we might have, would we take only the ordinary pains which are bestowed upon any of the comforts of life.

In all climates, fruit is of vast importance, but in a hot climate it is not merely a luxury, it is a real necessity. We have introduced into a country corresponding in thermal lines with the south of France and Italy all the habits of England and the north of Europe. Our houses are still built, our rooms still ventilated, our light and shade still disposed upon English models; and above all our tables are loaded, even during the summer months, with heavy joints of every kind, instead of vegetables and fruits, the proper diet of a warm climate. We ought to look to the East for our lessons in building and gardening and dietetics, and we should find in the courts and fountains and densely shaded gardens, in the frequent ablutions and frugal fruit diet of the East, the wise lessons which nature has taught the Asiatics, in the thousands of years of their experience; and if we had fruit in such abundance and of such a size and quality as we might possess it, we should soon find nature teaching us to substitute for traditional plum pudding and princely sirloins, vegetables and fruit, and thus add ten years to the average of human life. God has provided these things for us in rich abundance, just at the seasons when the animal economy most requires them, and has left us to animal food during those seasons when it can be digested with ease and healthfulness. All that is asked of us to respond to the indications of Providence and take due care that these things be properly cultivated and matured. Nothing is more wholesome than fine, well ripened fruit—nothing more unwholesome than the hard, knotty, half-ripe productions that are too often permitted to degrade the sacred names of peaches, apples and pears.

Each zone of climate has its peculiar fruits—those which it brings to highest perfection. Belgium and France seem to be the home of the pear and the plum;[15] Italy of the orange and olive; our Northern and North-Western States are peculiarly adapted to the apple;[16] and in like manner the peach and the melon flourish best in Georgia and Carolina. In these our State ought to stand unrivaled, and yet there are, perhaps, no two varieties of fruit in which there exists greater confusion, making it exceedingly difficult for an amateur to know what he possesses, and subjecting him to useless expense in procuring from abroad what he already has in higher luxuriance. We cannot progress, because we do not know where we stand; and like the young gentlemen who, after a wine party, unhappily stumbled upon a race course and traveled until morning upon a well beaten road which they were satisfied was taking them rapidly home—we are ever treading in our pomology, the same eternal circuit, you giving me under one name the same fruit which I have returned to you under another. Until some order shall be introduced into this matter and some attention paid to the comparison and naming of fruits within the State, we shall know neither our riches nor our poverty.

We possess in Georgia a great many fine peaches, but whether they are really new varieties or whether they are well known species modified by climate and soil, we have no means of ascertaining. Our Indian peach, for example, the most curious of our peaches, is scarcely noticed by Downing, and one would hardly detect our favorite under the title of "Columbia," which, as well as I can divine, is the name under which he describes it. Our Tinsley peach, a most decided favorite, is certainly a Georgia fruit, and we know it only in this neighborhood in its perfection.* What is called in Georgia the English peach, is probably a peach brought into Georgia from Virginia by some of the early settlers, who derived it from the mother country, and in almost every good orchard may be found several local varieties, having merely local names, and which it is almost impossible to compare with any foreign varieties because of the effect which climate has exerted upon them. Along with these we have a large variety of imported peaches, which are answering, under proper culture, the warmest encomiums of their owners. In my own experience, I would mention George IV, Crawford's early and late Melacatune, Bergen's yellow, the Oldmixon cling, and upon the recommendation of the Rev. Mr. Johnson, of Talbaton, Van Zandt's superb, as varieties richly repaying cultivation. Drs. Ward[17] and Camak[18] of Athens, whose names are known wherever pomology is cared for in the South, have recommended to me "La Bell de Beaucarie" as a peach surpassing, under their cultivation, all others they have tried. What we most need are good early and late peaches, so as to give a succession of good fruit. A peach was sent me by Corse, of Baltimore, under the name of Duff's Yellow, which seemed to answer, in some measure, the demand for an early peach. It ripened as early as the 4th of July— a very fine and large fruit—a full fortnight before any of the finer Northern peaches came to maturity. It seems, from its name, to be a local peach and I would remark, in passing, that the gardens of Baltimore would probably very much enrich our circle of peaches, inasmuch as their soil is very like that of middle Georgia, and their latitude some degrees nearer our own than that of New York or Boston. A fine late peach has probably been found, but it has yet to be tested by a larger experience.

*It is probably the same as the Pace Peach of our Eastern Counties.

In the middle and upper parts of Georgia we are not much troubled with the common enemies of the peach. A little care in searching the roots for the borer seems to be almost all that is necessary in our climate and soil, where the trees have been properly planted in the first instance and are kept clear from weeds and grass. Should the worm become troublesome, the freedom of the orchard given to the hogs will soon remedy the evil. But there is one neglect which injures our peach orchards more than every thing else, and that is the superabundant product which is permitted to form and strive after maturity. We see most of our Georgia peach orchards broken down and rendered worthless for want of a little care at the proper season. The preventives for this mischief are the shortening in system and the removal of the inferior fruit so soon as it sufficiently develops itself to mark its inferiority. For a few years you will have less fruit, but it will be better and your orchard continue in fine bearing years after that of your careless neighbor shall have been destroyed and cut up.

I would recommend to every farmer in Georgia the practice of planting the stone of every peach that deserves the trouble. By adopting this method a constant succession of trees would be secured and new seedlings be produced adding to our list of excellent peaches. These stones should be planted very soon after the fruit has been eaten, and label attached, designating in every instance, as far as possible, the fruit whence the stone was taken.

The Water Melon requires scarcely any cultivation further than the choice of good seed and a location where it may be freed from too much damp and moisture. Its peculiar home seems to be the sandy soil of the sea Islands; and it loves nothing so well as to repose its sleek sides in a heated bed of sand, which the bare foot of the white man could scarcely tolerate. It is almost incredible, what a size they attain, and what a richness of flavor, under such conditions; and I suppose the water melon could scarcely be improved by importations of seeds. Our musk melons and cantalopes are far inferior to our water melons, and need the attention of the lovers of good fruit. They might be very much improved by importations of seed from abroad, especially when we know that there are seventy kinds named upon the catalogue of the London Horticultural Society.

The Apricot, the Nectarine, the Plum, are scarcely known in Georgia. Here and there a few are produced; but the unceasing and almost irremediable ravages of the curculio, and the slovenly manner in which we have cultivated all our fruit, have made them exceedingly rare—rarer than they should be, I think; for while I despair of raising these smooth skinned fruits in the open field culture which we give to the peach and the apple, I think they may be produced upon a smaller scale. They have been matured in great perfection in South Carolina and Georgia, and why may they not be again.

The finest nectarines I have ever seen, were produced in the paved yards of the city of Charleston—yards closely and entirely paved, and swept daily of all the offal of the tree. They attained a large size, a delicious flavor, and were entirely free from the curculio. This is an isolated fact, and yet worth recording; for it is one step in the process of induction. The best apricots I have ever eaten were grown, in like manner, in close proximity to the dwelling house, upon a spot where the soil was trodden upon every day, until it was as hard as brick, and the offal was carefully removed. This is a like fact, affording another step in our induction. The finest plums and gages I have ever met with at the south were all grown upon dwarfed trees, forming heads which sheltered their bark, and planted in courts and yards trodden continually by the foot of man, and freely reached by brooms and poultry. These facts, coming under my own observation, in every case where I have remarked these fruits to be peculiarly fine, have fixed my belief, in spite of the pros and cons of the books, that the true remedy for the curculio is the neighborhood of the household, the use of the broom, and the freedom of the manor to the poultry, and perchance a few genteel pigs, taught by a ring in the nose not to do more than skim the surface of the soil. Such a proximity as this, joined to a constant dwarfing of the trees, so as to protect their bark, especially in the case of the apricot, might afford some remedy to this evil.

Another suggestion has been made to me by Mr. Carolan, my gardener at Montpelier, which may be deserving of attention. He observed that the curculio did not destroy the native and common plums of the country, especially where they were grown in dense masses, as plum orchards are usually permitted to grow. The plums, under such circumstances were inferior in size, but free from worms. Might not this thick planting and dense shading of the surface of the earth help us to the solution of this problem? And should we be satisfied of this, might we not secure the shade and coldness of earth necessary to disturb and discourage the curculio, without sacrificing the proper size of the fruit, by planting our smooth skinned fruits on the north side of walls and buildings? It may be that this little pirate may require a certain amount of light and heat to make his abode comfortable, and that, failing all other hints, we may freeze him out by depriving him of the comforts of life. Every thing deserves to be considered in connection with this pest, and I throw out this suggestion for as much as it is worth. Should every thing else fail, these fruits may be grown in boxes, and matured under the shelter of the green house.

The Pear has hitherto been a very scarce fruit in Georgia owing to two causes. First, because it is a tree of very slow growth, requiring a long time to bring it into bearing; and secondly, because it is a very delicate tree with us, requiring a great deal of peculiar care and attention. The results, therefore, have not been at all adequate to the efforts which have been made, and ill success has produced something like despair. But these causes are yielding to the more permanent settlement of the country, and to the undisputed and eminent success which has attended the culture of this fruit in and around Athens. The gardens of Dr. Ward and the late Mr. Camak, of Athens, prove beyond a question, the complete adaptation of upper Georgia to the culture of the pear; and all that is now needed is to ascertain the varieties which seem best suited to the climate and soil of Georgia. This is of vast importance, for it is well known that varieties of apple and pear are first rate only in particular localities; and that a distance of a hundred miles will produce such a change as to modify very much the quality of the fruit. It is all important therefore, when we are about to commence the cultivation of this fruit, that we should import varieties which have succeeded, and avoid the mortification of finding, at the end of ten years, that the choice varieties of the books were not those which suited us best. Was I about to commence this culture, I should infinitely prefer taking the advice of such gentlemen as had practically tested the matter, rather than depend upon the recommendations of the catalogues, or the decisions of pomological conventions where the South had not been represented.

It is scarcely necessary to touch upon the cultivation of the apple. It is so favorite a fruit, is so universally cultivated, and is produced of such good size and flavor in many parts of the State, that attention is sufficiently excited about it, and large importations are constantly being made of the most approved varieties. The important points in the apple culture are, to test and note the results of these importations, and to endeavor to find an apple that will keep during our winter months. Until we make this discovery we shall be tributary for this useful fruit.

Nothing proves more conclusively our subservience to the North and to England, in our horticulture, than our neglect of the Fig. Because it is a fruit denied to them, with meek submission, we have concluded that we will deny it to ourselves. This is true only of the middle and upper parts of Georgia. In the lower country, it has so forced itself upon the notice of the people, that they have condescended to cultivate it; but even with them very little pains has been taken to introduce the finest varieties. No fruit is more delicious, more wholesome, or more certain in its returns, and yet in Georgia only a few varieties of this fruit are generally cultivated. The horticulturists of the eastern shore of Georgia ought to take care that the best varieties of the Mediterranean and Levant are placed within our reach. In our middle section of the State it is a fruit almost entirely neglected; and yet so far north as Atlanta it requires only a moderate protection. If carefully guarded for a few years, it will assimilate itself; and it often happens that the frosts which seriously injure the figs of the seaboard and the Gulf, do not affect us. And the solution is a very simple one. The early warmth of February in those latitudes, causes the tree to move its sap and prepare for growth, foliage and fruit. In this condition the frosts of February and March find it, and a severe check is the consequence. The same cold finds our trees still in the repose of winter, and expends itself upon a mass prepared to meet it. Extreme seasons, such as '27 or '35, would of course put the fig to a severe trial; but as these terrible frosts are but rare, and the fig is a tree of rapid growth, they are not worth taking into the account. My own trees stood entirely uninjured the cold of 1848, when the thermometer declined to 8°. But in this latitude they must be protected for a winter or two, during their early growth; and no better covering can be found for them than the common broom-sedge of the old fields, tied closely around them, and giving them the appearance of a wheat or rye stack. Should any persons desire to cultivate the fig, I would recommend them, for the present, to procure cuttings from the seaboard of Georgia and Carolina, where a few fine varieties are in cultivation. The blue and the brown figs are the best.

The various berries which make such a delicious appendage to the dessert—the Strawberry, the Raspberry, the Blackberry—are at last beginning to receive attention among us. Mr. Peabody, of Columbus, has opened a new era in the strawberry culture; and his wonderful success in quantity, in size, in flavor, has attracted attention every where. He has achieved the wonderful feat of furnishing this fruit in profusion, from April to October. With such a master at the head of the horticultural department of the Soil of the South,[19] it would be presumption for any one to speak of the culture of this fruit, and I will therefore only say, that the secrets of its culture are, a due intermixture of staminate and pistillate plants, the use of vegetable rather than animal manures, mulching with tan or dried leaves, or straw, or even broom-sedge, and abundant watering during the season of fructification. Hovey's Seedling is incomparably the best variety I know. This intermingled with the large Early Scarlet, or the Boston Pine, will give very fine and abundant fruit.

The common variety of the black Raspberry, commonly called the Thimbleberry, produces very freely in middle and upper Georgia. But the finer varieties of red and yellow Antwerp, and Fastolff, are with us very shy bearers. Whether sufficient pains have not been taken with their cultivation, or whether the climate is too hot for them, they certainly are as rare among us as gages or apricots. I have never been able to do more than procure enough merely to say that they had been raised. But their cultivation in more northern parts of the State might be eminently successful.

The Blackberry is one of the fruits which we ought to improve by artificial means. Our wild blackberries are, in many cases, very large and well flavored; and there is no telling how delicious a fruit might not be produced by its careful cultivation. It is a subject worthy the attention of our horticulturists.

I suppose it may create a smile in this audience, when I recommend that the like efforts should be made with the Persimmon. It is, even in its wild state, a very palatable fruit, and might become, under high cultivation, a very delightful addition to the dessert. I venture to affirm, that if our eastern friends possessed it, with the advantages we have of climate and soil, we should soon hear of it as large as a peach, and receive it, in rich abundance, as a substitute for dates and dried figs. We leave it for the hogs; they would very soon make it a fruit to grace the table of a prince.

The culture of the Grape is at a very low ebb in Georgia. With the exception of the smooth skinned fruits, I know nothing so rare as a dish of good grapes. Even the coarser grapes of the country are by no means a certain crop; and with the exception of the Scuppernong, none can be counted upon in every season. The grape seems to need, more than any fruit I know, a certain combination of circumstances; and when these meet, it is as prolific and as certain as our blackberry. When I walked over the vineyards around Cincinnati, rising terrace above terrace, to the very summit of their hills, and saw the luxurious clusters hanging by wagon loads upon their vigorous stocks, I could not but feel that it was not cultivation but soil, climate, location, which made the vast difference. The very same varieties of grape had been cultivated with infinite pains in Georgia, but had not at all repaid their cultivators, scarcely furnishing enough for the use of the table, far less the wine-press. For any thing like wine culture, the banks of the Tennessee, from Knoxville to the Muscle Shoals, offer, in my opinion, the finest field, with the best prospect of success. The vine seems to love the neighborhood of rivers where they are flanked by hills of moderate height, or even by mountains, and can find the drainage and nutriment necessary for its successful growth.

But while we may be denied the grape for its wine, it is entirely within our power to have it, at very little cost, in abundance as a table fruit. We speak of the vine clad hills of France, and we speak truly, but the table grapes of France are not comparable to those which are raised in England by artificial means, where the outdoor culture has been long abandoned. These artificial means are entirely within our reach at far less expense than in England, and there is no farmer of any enterprise, who might not have an abundance of the finest table grapes of the world, at no other cost than a little pains in gaining information and putting it in practice. For the last two years I have been running the Black Hamburgh, the Muscat of Alexandria, the Chasselas, and other foreign grapes, upon the rafters of my green house, and the past summer they bore very fine fruit, which came to high perfection. The only trouble was the preparation of the border, and this a little labor can effect.

But it may be said, we have no green houses, and we cannot afford to build them. That may be so, although I by no means admit the expensiveness of a green house, but even for this there is no necessity. Any body who can put up a log cabin can put up such a house as is necessary for grape culture in Georgia. It is not, as in England, the artificial heat that we need, which requires glass, and flues, and all the expensive apparatus of vineries; it is simply protection from the excessive changes which distinguish our American from the European climate. To meet this single difficulty I would suggest a building exactly like a vinery in form and shape except that it be built of the rudest materials, logs put together and the interstices closed with clay, while the sides and front and top be covered with frames of oiled homespun, such as were recommended for the pit culture of tender exotics. The poles or rafters extending from the front to the rear should be four feet apart, and about six inches in width. From a border made outside the house, pass the vines in and run them upon these rafters, and with the proper preparation of the soil, which any of the books will give, and the proper management of the vines, the finest grapes may be matured. The frames which fit in between the rafters should be well jointed and connected by hinges with the rear, and furnished with cords and pullies for raising them for ventilation and sun. In forming the border be not carried away with the vulgar idea of stuffing it with animal manure. Nothing will so soon and certainly disgust the delicate feeders of the roots of the vine.

Besides these fruits of ordinary culture in Georgia, there is a large family of the Aurantaceae, which deserve a passing notice, as capable of profitable cultivation upon the sea coast. The Orange, the Lemon, the Lime, the Citron, the Shaddock can all be raised upon the eastern coast of Georgia with great profit; and while, for the present, the prospect of the Orange crop is clouded by the ravages of an insect, we trust, from what we learn, that it has run its course and is now passing away. As far north as the islands of Hilton Head, Port Royal and St. Helena, in South Carolina, the Orange and Lemon bear profusely, in the open air, and although they cannot bear our most excessive frosts, the only fatal year in this century has been the cold of 1835. There are now very large groves, one numbering, upon Cumberland Island, as many as two thousand trees, awaiting the departure of the insect. It would be well for those who are engaged in the cultivation of this family of plants to import the best works upon this natural order from France and Italy, so that they may choose among the varieties for culture. The most valuable works are those by Dr. Sickler*, Gallesio†, and Risso and Poisseau§, expensive and in foreign languages, but still very necessary for the proper understanding of the genus Citrus. A very valuable addition might be made to our resources by turning these fruits into sweetmeats and exporting them to the North and Europe.

Besides this family of Mediterranean and Eastern culture, there are other fruits which deserve the attention of the sea coast of Georgia, and are receiving it. The Olive can be cultivated with complete success, and if the oil taste could only be created in the United States, might form a very lucrative branch of horticulture. The Date has been matured upon St. Simon's Island. A bunch I think is now on exhibition within these walls, and the Guava will stand most of the winters of south eastern Georgia and Florida. We should never forget that our most valuable staples, our rice, our cotton, our wheat, were all introduced from abroad, and that the food of the lower classes of Great Britain and much of Europe is an American root. Who can place any bounds to the adaptation of such a climate as we possess, for really as between the mountains of Rabun and Dade and the ocean washed shores of our islands, we embrace almost every variety of atmosphere which floats between Canada and Cuba.

Closely connected with these two branches of horticulture, is the art of Landscape Gardening, in which we are more deficient than in

\* Der vollkemmen orangerie. Gartner, 1815.
† Traite du Genre Citrus. Savonna, 1818.
§ Historie Naturelle des orangers par Risso at Poisseau. Paris Folio, 1818.

any thing else. With all the advantages which nature can give us, we have none of the appliances of art. Our houses, with some exceptions, exhibit the most wretched specimens of architecture, our out-houses are arranged just in the most conspicuously awkward positions, our orchards are where our ornamental grounds should be, and our vegetable gardens thrust up their tall collards and peasticks where the rose and the jasmine ought to be taught to twine. And all this, too, not from any necessity in the case; it is a mere matter of bad taste. A well proportioned house, in good keeping in its arrangements and ornaments, is not more expensive than such outre models as stare at us along our roads; and where land is plentiful, it makes no sort of difference in expense as to the location of the outbuildings or of the various gardens. There is no man, of any property, who could not afford to preserve around his dwelling woodland enough to make a grove and lawn for shade, for comfort and for ornament. Was this always observed in the settlement of new places, what a different aspect would our country soon present! Instead of bare red hills, crowned with great white houses glaring at you through the broiling sun and making heat even hotter, surrounded by negro quarters of the most ungainly aspect, with cotton and corn growing up to the very doors, we should have a variety of pretty country seats, or neat farm houses, peeping out of parks and groves, with lawns sweeping down to the entrance gate, and with pleasant associations all around. As one approached the seat of wealth and refinement, instead of a straight up and down clay road, flanked by straggling Virginia fences[20] on either hand, and ornamented as you approach the house by consumptive hogs wallowing in the dirty puddles they have made before the very door, we should find a winding road running through native forest trees until it came out upon the ornamental gardens of the estate, and opening, as it wound towards the mansion, picturesque objects at every turn. Instead of rude log cabins, and dirty negroes grinning at you from every door, distance would be taught to lend enchantment to the view, even of these appendages of necessity.

Instead of discomfort and filth and the offal of a yard heaped all around you, you would find the education and refinement and wealth of the inhabitants fairly represented in their abodes, and "beautiful as apples of gold in pictures of silver." It is sickening, as one passes through the middle counties of Georgia, to behold its deformed appearance. Naturally it is one of the most beautiful countries in the world, for nothing is more picturesque than the alternation of hill and dale, the undulating sweep of a rolling country, the variety of foliage that arises from the intermixture of so many species of forest trees; but as man has dealt with it, it is rapidly becoming one of the ugliest. For it is the peculiarity of a rolling country, whose subsoil is red clay, to be either very beautiful or very ugly. The elements of beauty are likewise the elements of its ugliness—the curve line of beauty, unless preserved, rapidly breaking into the rugged wrinkles of an early decrepitude, and the clay that would, with due treatment, have afforded sustenance to a lawn of velvet, running speedily into a surface of baked brick. But sad as has been the havoc, it is not yet too late; much of the woodland is yet untouched; many of the hills are yet crowned with their primeval forest; and thanks to the progress of refinement, many of the newly opened estates in upper Georgia have been arranged with a view to ornament as well as profit—have mingled the idea of the beautiful with the sense of the practical.

Two thirds of the year, in our climate, is a conflict with heat. Every thing, therefore, which art can do ought to be done to mitigate its fervor and make life comfortable. And yet, strange to say, very little is done towards that end. Our houses are built with small porches, giving no protection to their sides, instead of deep piazzas and graceful verandahs through which the winds may play and cool themselves before they kiss our cheeks. Every native tree is swept down before the relentless axe, as if to court the sun, and in their places are gradually reared, with infinite pains, prim rows of Lombardy poplars, or groups of stunted altheas, or perchance a straggling tree of Heaven, that certainly has got out of Paradise. Nothing there that may produce shade or modify the glare and heat of the sun. No trees, casting their sweet foliage, like the shadow of a great rock in a weary land, over the roof; no vines creeping up and sheltering the sides; no shrubs intercepting the air and loading it with freshness and perfume as it passes on its errand of mercy. All is one broad glare of heat, searing the eyes, filling the atmosphere with a reflection hotter than the reality, and every day preparing within the house a furnace for the night. And as it is with our houses so is it with our grounds. We seem to forget that the direct heat of the sun is only a portion of that which we are called to bear; that every thing reflects heat, and that a surface of sand or clay will give out an infinitely larger portion of it than a surface of dew moistened and densely matted grass. But where are our lawns? Where are the green spots that are to relieve the eye and cheer the exhausted nature? There are literally none. A green sward is almost as rare in Georgia as a pavement of jasper. Not only is art seldom applied for this purpose, but nature is not permitted to do even the little which she desires.

One of the chief beauties of England, the most gorgeously cultivated country of the world, consists in what is called her park scenery and in her lawns. In plain language this means nothing more than such a disposition of trees and grass as shall best satisfy the eye of a man of taste. Now I do not mean to say that we could, by any process, rival the richness of the English parks and lawns, and for the single reason that we lack the dull skies and the humid atmosphere and the frequent rains of the sea girt isles; but an humble imitation and a distant approach would certainly be better than fields of broomsedge and rows of withered cornstalks. And that approach we can make either by artificial or natural means. Let us consider both briefly.

If the desire is to have a perfect lawn, pains and labor will have to be bestowed upon it. Deep spading, a free use of lime where it does not exist in the soil, clean weeding, nice harrowing, a mixture of blue grass, white clover and English lawn seed rolled in plaster before planting, constant top dressings of plaster or charcoal, all these will be necessary, not once but often, to enable it to stand the heat of our suns, and the interminable droughts of our summers. What lawn, however prepared, could bear such a spring, summer and autumn as we have just passed through? But we must not reason from extremes and refuse to enjoy our many ordinary years, because an extraordinary one may intervene and blight our labor. In land prepared and dressed as above recommended a very fair lawn can be obtained. The white clover protects the other grasses for two or three years and then dies out leaving them to form the smooth body of the sward. To the labor above detailed must be added frequent scything and rolling with a heavy stone roller. All weeds and intrusive grasses must be carefully handpicked until you shall have destroyed all that was left in the original preparation of the soil. The seed ought to be placed in such a lawn by October, so as to give it a firm root and a steady growth before the trying heats of summer.

This is the artificial method, but there is one much more simple by which in two or three years nature will do the work and keep it done. Let me suppose that you have preserved around your dwelling some fifty or sixty acres of woodland, out of which you desire to make a park. Your first process would be to take out all the decayed and deformed trees and destroy them. Underbrushing would succeed to this and then a cleaning out of stumps and roots and the offal of the wood. When the surface shall have been rendered smooth, then take out the poorest and ugliest and most unpromising of the remaining trees so as to let in the sun and light in moderate degree upon the surface of the soil. This done, you have an open wood with a surface covered with fallen leaves. And here begins the lesson taught us by the Indians who preceded us in the possession of this fair country. They left us, when they ceded middle Georgia to us, one of the loveliest lands on which the eye could rest—long sweeps of open woodland, undulating and covered as far as the eye can reach with waving grass; no underbrush, no rubbish, but a rolling wooded prairie, such as may be seen, ere the white man utterly ruins it, in Illinois and Indiana. To produce this result Indian used *fire* and you must imitate his example. So soon as your leaves are dry enough to kindle put in fire and reduce the whole surface to ashes. Out of this grave will spring up what you are looking for, a native grass that will give you in a few years of repetition a very pretty sward, provided you will use the scythe upon it freely. This will not be, of course, such a lawn as the artificial one I have described, but it will afford a most delightful relief to the eye, and, covered with fine cattle, will give an idea, at least, of the English lawn.

Although I have already trespassed upon your patience, I must be permitted to add a few words upon the subject of Hedges. So long as the straggling Virginia fence is adhered to, and indeed any fence except it be an invisible one of wire, we shall always have a blot upon our landscapes. To obviate this we should every where substitute hedges, especially in the room of inner fences, such as surround and protect our dwellings and our gardens. We rejoice in an abundance of material for such an hedge. We have the cedar, the holly, the Cherokee, white microphilla and macartney roses, the privet, the osage orange, and in the lower country the cassina. Any of these form beautiful hedges, and are adapted for outer or inner fences according as one may desire.

Of these the cedar and the holly are evergreens, which gives them a vast superiority over the others. For inner hedges they should be always employed; but for outer hedges the osage orange and the white microphylla rose are unrivaled. Both these plants are vigorous growers, presenting an almost impenetrable barrier of wood and thorns against any assailant, and from April to November presenting to the eye a mass of richest green. They are both produced easily from cuttings—the osage orange from cuttings both of the branches and roots. I prefer the white microphylla rose very much to the cherokee, as it possesses all its good qualities and is not so straggling above nor ragged below. For planting out objects the macartney rose stands supreme; and for delicate tracery the privet and cassina are the most beautiful.

Before I close I would beg permission to suggest a few practical modes of elevating our horticultural position and taking our proper place among the societies which now grace almost every State. We have hitherto done very little systematically, let us strive now to gather and concentrate the individual energy which is toiling without sympathy and without countenance.

1. We have established in Macon a Central Horticultural Society for the State.[21] Let this be the society around which shall spring up branch societies in all the towns of Georgia. Savannah, Columbus, Augusta, Athens and Milledgeville, are full of amateurs who need only the bond of a society to make them eminently useful. Let me urge it upon those cities to take the matter in hand and to form local societies which shall send up annually delegates to this central society to compare progress, interchange experience and promote the great ends of our union. While we should thus awaken a proper spirit in these localities, we should likewise act, through the Central Association, in harmony about all those points in which harmony is so requisite.

2. Let those Branch Societies, and the Central Society, invite at their meetings, literary contributions from their members upon points connected with Horticulture, details of interesting experiments, successful culture of particular flowers, fruits or vegetables, production of new varieties, etc. Let these papers be subject to the control of the Executive Committee of the respective societies, who shall publish such of them as they may deem important in some one of the agricultural papers of the State.

3. The arrangement of quarterly exhibitions in all these societies,

and a general one of such things as may bear transportation at the annual State Fair. The winter exhibition should be for exotics; say camellias, azaleas, epiphyllums, etc. The spring exhibition for roses, hyacinths, tulips, amaryllis, together with such fruits as may mature at that season. The summer for all flowers belonging to that season, and for peaches, nectarine, etc. The fall may be merged in the Central State Fair, and include particularly apples and pears. The most suitable months, in our climate, would be the end of January and beginning of February for the winter exhibition; the end of April and beginning of May for the spring exhibition; the end of July and beginning of August for the summer. The period of the State Fair is probably now settled for this month.

4. The last means for the promotion of horticulture among ourselves, is the encouragement of nursery gardens at home. For the long and tedious experiments which are necessary for the determining of many points in Horticulture, a permanent establishment is necessary; one in which results can be noted over a long series of years and time be allowed for the testing of fruits, vegetables and flowers. To a certain extent this may be achieved by individuals, but not so perfectly as in nursery gardens. Besides, it is so convenient and such an encouragement to amateurs to have an establishment at hand where such things can be procured at little trouble and without the expense of agencies. Many a person would be deterred from improving his grounds or orchards by the difficulty of obtaining trees and plants from a distance, while if they were near at hand, he would often be tempted, without any previous inclination, to embark in the matter of Horticulture. Let every Horticulturist determine, therefore, as a duty which he owes to the science, to encourage the nursery gardens nearest to him and to cheer on those engaged in the enterprise. Such things must have their beginning every where, and if we intend to make a new era in the science, we must purchase every thing at

home that can be obtained. The result will be, that from the superiority of climate and soil, much finer plants can be furnished at the same price, and plants too having the advantage of being acclimated, and without the risk of removal. It might be a matter of consideration with the Horticultural Societies how far they would encourage beginners by loans of money and temporary assistance; for it requires some years before a nursery garden can be made profitable. It is very gratifying to me to be able to state that such nurseries are springing up in the neighborhood of our principal towns, and promise in time to be useful and profitable.

I have not deemed it necessary, in an address like this, to prove the advantages, the uses, or the enjoyments of horticulture. I have taken these points for granted, and have proceeded in my discussion upon the grounds that my audience fully agreed with me in those respects. I may have been too sanguine in my conclusions; and if I have, must beg you to pardon my mistake, for it has arisen only out of my own ardent love for every thing connected with the beauties of nature. It was born with me; it has grown with my growth, and strengthened with my advancing life; it has been a source of health, of contentment, of rich enjoyment to me; and in the midst of cares and responsibilities of no ordinary nature, I have always found relief from the pressure of thought and the burden of anxiety in my gardens and among my flowers. It has opened before me higher views of the beneficence of my Creator, and has taught me the important lesson—a lesson which cannot be too much impressed upon an utilitarian age—that over and above the useful, the profitable, the necessary, God has deemed it wise to surround his creatures with the beautiful, the picturesque, the sublime. Let us imitate his wisdom, and while we neglect none of the duties of life, nor evade any of its responsibilities, let us surround ourselves and our children with those rich appliances of nature and art which gratify the taste, which elevate the feelings, which teach us to look from nature up to nature's God. Like all the highest blessings of his providence—the air, the water, the sun—God has placed flowers and fruits within the reach of every one of his creatures, and there is no homestead so poor, no plot of ground so small, but that it may be made with a little labor and a little care redolent with beauty and perfume. May the time soon come, when over the length and breadth of the land we shall find taste, beauty, ornament mingled with the necessities of life, and a glory of art corresponding in some measure with the glory of nature—when man shall aspire to imitate his Maker, and beautify rather than disfigure the great temple wherein he has placed us for worship, amid the richness of his own tracery and the grandeur of his own handiwork.

# NOTES

Bishop Elliott was speaking to a Georgia (and Southern) audience of the 1850's and the people who composed this group knew the significance of his reference to the people, places and events of that period. Realizing that these references have no particular meaning to the average reader of the address in the 1940's, I am including the following explanatory notes. I owe my thanks to Professor James C. Bonner, Head, Department of History, Georgia State College for Women, Milledgeville, Georgia, for valuable suggestions and assistance in compiling these notes; Mr. Robert W. B. Elliott, Sewanee, Tennessee, grandson of Bishop Elliott; and Mr. J. Freeman Hart, Macon, Georgia, the present owner of Montpelier, for information and source data.

H. B. O.

*1* In August, 1846, a group of leading citizens of Georgia met at Stone Mountain and organized the South Central Agricultural Society in the belief "that great good may result to the planting interests of Georgia, Carolina, Alabama, and Tennessee from a personal interchange of the results of their experience, accompanied (when convenient) by an exhibition of the products of their farms and plantations." The first four Fairs (exhibitions) of this Society in 1846, 1847, 1848, and 1849 were held at Stone Mountain; that of 1850 at Atlanta; and that of 1851 in Macon. The Secretary of the Society, in the published transactions for 1851, states "the meeting at Macon was the most brilliant of its kind in every respect ever held in the South." The city of Macon gave the Society $2,000 to be used for premiums. In addition to this sum, $4,178.73 was realized as the amount of receipts for the Fair of 1851.

*2* The prospectus of the school for the year 1849 shows that the Boys' Department had been discontinued, and the name became the Montpelier Female Institute. It indicates that there were school rooms, music rooms, drawing rooms, painting rooms, chemical and physical laboratories, green-houses, and a chapel with a seating capacity of one hundred and fifty. The two largest buildings used as dormitories and class rooms, were Lamar Hall and Chase Hall. At a meeting of the Board of Trustees in December, 1855, it was unanimously determined to close the Montpelier Institute and thus ended Bishop Elliott's connection with the school. After going into private hands it was operated for some years by Prof. C. B. Martin, later by Rev. Pryse, and finally by Prof. Ben Polhill. Prof. Polhill's School for Boys is well remembered by people in Macon and middle Georgia today. The Professor died in 1876, and three years later the property was acquired by the Hart family. Lamar Hall, a two-story structure of twenty

[ 52 ]

two rooms, became the Hart family residence. That building was destroyed by fire several years ago. Today Mr. J. Freeman Hart, of Macon, has a country home at Montpelier, built on the original site of Lamar Hall. The Chapel and the walls of Chase Hall still stand as reminders of Bishop Elliott's stewardship of the school one hundred years ago.

*3* Robert Nelson, a native of Denmark who came to Georgia in the 1840's as a result of the revolutionary ferment in Europe. His father is said to have been "one of the most extensive, if not the largest practical farmer and stockholder on the European continent." Robert Nelson was educated in European Universities and, despite his accent, he was much respected throughout the Lower South for his excellent conversation, good common sense, and horticultural skill. He acquired 95 acres of land near Macon and established the Troup Hill Nursery. By the time of the Civil War he had removed to Montgomery, Alabama, and was horticultural editor of the *American Cotton Planter and Soil of the South.*

*4* Claude, or Claude Lorrain (1600-1682), whose real name was Claude Gellee. French landscape painter whose works, along with those of Poussin and Salvator Rosa, greatly influenced the development of the informal style of landscape gardening in England in the 18th and 19th centuries.

*5* One-third of Georgia's total area was taken from the Creek and Cherokee Indians between 1825 and 1838. The ceded area included the land between the Flint and Chattahoochee rivers and that portion of the Cherokee Nation in northwest Georgia. In 1844 the state announced the final disposal of all of its public lands.

*6* In 1811, under the national plan for improvements, a "Federal Highway" was built from Milledgeville westward to the Chattahoochee river near the present site of Columbus. This road was extended westward to the Mississippi river and became the main route of travelers to the Southwest.

*7* At this time no book dealing with landscape gardening or fruit growing in the South had been written. Elliott was undoubtedly familiar with works on these subjects by northern and European authors, i.e.: A. J. Downing, *A Treatise on the Theory and Practice of Landscape Gardening* (New York, 1841); *Cottage Residences* (New York, 1842); *The Fruits and Fruit Trees of North America* (New York, 1845); Patrick Barry, *The Fruit Garden* (New York, 1851), and others.

*8* Agricultural societies did not come into existence in Georgia until after 1840. In the decade which followed, several were organized in Middle Georgia, the most prominent being the Hancock Planter's Club at Sparta. In the same decade the *Southern Cultivator* was established at Augusta. This was the only southern agricultural journal which survived the Civil War, and it achieved a notable reputation throughout the country.

*9* Elliott was probably referring to "Gloaming Nursery" at Clarkesville. Established in the late 1840's by Jarvis Van Buren (1801-1885), it was said to be the first nursery in Georgia. Van Buren early recognized the horticultural possibilities of Georgia and he assembled the largest collection of southern seedling apples ever seen in the South. He was a prolific contributor to agricultural journals and did pioneer work in developing a commercial apple industry in North Georgia.

*10* The Camellia (Camellia japonica), Tea Rose (Rosa odorata), Crape Myrtle (Lagerstromea indica), Azalea (Azalea indica), Oleander (Nerium oleander) and Gardenia (Gardenia florida) are native to Asia. The Oleander is also indigenous to the Mediterranean region of Africa and Europe, and one species of Gardenia is found in South Africa.

*11* Louis LeConte (1782-1838), a planter and scientist who lived at Woodmanston plantation in Liberty County, Georgia. He developed a botanical and floral garden there which included many rare specimens of plants. His beautiful garden became celebrated all over the United States, and botanists from the North and from Europe came to visit it. He was the father of Joseph LeConte, an eminent professor and scientist.

*12* Sir Joseph Paxton (1801-1865), an English architect and horticulturist who erected a great conservatory for the Duke of Devonshire at Chatsworth, Derbyshire.

*13* These two roses were hybridized in the vicinity of Charleston and bear the names of their originators.

*14* Charles Alfred Peabody was a pioneer in southern strawberry culture. Solon Robinson called him the most successful strawberry culturist in the world. By 1857 he was shipping the fruit from his farm near Columbus to every market town of importance in the United States where it arrived in advance of any other available supply. Unknown as a southern fruit before Peabody's day, it soon threatened the monopoly of the Cincinnati growers. A prominent horticultural editor in Alabama and Georgia, Peabody also made some valuable contributions to southern floriculture and landscape gardening.

*15* In 1857 Prosper Jules Alphonse Berckmans acquired Fruitland Nursery at Augusta where, with his father, Louis E. Berckmans, he began to popularize the growing of pears and plums in the Lower South. Born in 1830 at Arschot, Belgium, the younger Berckmans became one of the most noted horticulturists in the South. He was perhaps the disseminator of more original ornamental forms than any other Southerner. He was the only American to act as a judge at the Centennial of the Royal Agricultural Society in Ghent in 1908.

*16* At this time Elliott and the general public were not aware of the potentialities of apple-growing in North Georgia. It was not until about 1854 that Jarvis Van Buren succeeded in convincing southern editors and others that the Appalachian foothills of the South possessed great commercial apple-growing possibilities.

*17* Malthus A. Ward (1781-1863) of Salem, Massachusetts, was appointed professor of Natural History in the University of Georgia in 1831. During the two decades which followed he did more perhaps to introduce and disseminate fruits and flowers than any person in the state. He was responsible for the establishment of a botanical garden on the University Campus in 1833. It soon became one of the greatest attractions in Athens with more than 2,000 species of plants from every corner of the globe. As the garden grew in size, it became more expensive to maintain and finally, in 1856, when the trustees were unable to provide funds for this purpose, it was sold for $1,000.

*18* James Camak (1795-1847) was one of the builders of the Georgia Railroad, the first president of the Georgia Bank, and editor of the *Georgia Journal*. He founded the *Southern Cultivator* which he edited until his death. While interested primarily in horticulture, he conducted many valuable experiments on field crops as well. The father of Dr. James Camak (1822-1892), of Athens. The younger James Camak was a matriculate in the Class of 1841 at the University of Georgia, later graduating from Princeton University. Listed in Hull's *Alumni Record* (of the University of Georgia) as physician and horticulture editor. At the fifth annual Fair held by the South Central Agricultural Society in Atlanta, in August 1850, a year before Bishop Elliott made his address, Dr. Camak submitted the greatest variety of fruit in the Horticulture exhibit, for which he was awarded a silver cup. This exhibit embraced 45 varieties of pears, several varieties of apples, and "three most superb varieties of plums." The Committee on Horticulture reported that Dr. Camak cultivated the peach with great success, specimens of which were not submitted because of the distance of the orchard.

*19* An agricultural journal published at Columbus, Georgia, from 1851 to 1857.

*20* The Split rail fence commonly seen today in the North Georgia mountain area.

*21* Elliott was the first president of the Central Horticultural Association organized at Macon in 1849. Others prominent in its organization were Simri Rose, Iverson L. Harris, Robert Nelson, and James A. Nisbet. While its name suggested regional ambitions, it was never more than a local organization composed principally of men living at Macon and Milledgeville. Other local horticultural societies were later established at Athens, Augusta, and Atlanta.

BIOGRAPHICAL NOTE: Bishop Elliott was married twice and had eight children. His first wife was Mary Barnwell. To this union were born: (1) Stephen, and (2) Mary Elizabeth, who was married to William Carmichael of Deptford Plantation, situated just outside of Savannah. His second wife was Charlotte Bull Barnwell. Their children were: (3) Robert Woodward Barnwell, first Missionary Bishop of Texas. He married Caroline Elliott of Savannah. (4) John Barnwell, a physician, who married Harriott Lucas Huger. (5) Esther Habersham (Mrs. Francis Asbury Shoup). (6) Robert Habersham, a civil engineer. (7) Sarah Bull Barnwell, authoress, and (8) Charlotte Barnwell (Mrs. Charles McDonald Puckette).

# BIBLIOGRAPHY

Downing, Andrew Jackson, *A Treatise on the Theory and Practice of Landscape Gardening*. Riker, Thorne & Co., New York, N. Y., 1854.

Elliott, Rt. Rev. Stephen, Annual Address before Clariosophic & Euphradian Societies at the South Carolina College, (Pamphlet). Walker, Evans & Co., Charleston, S. C., 1860.

Elliott, Rt. Rev. Stephen, A Sermon—"Humiliation, Fasting, and Prayer," (Pamphlet). Steam Power Press of John M. Cooper & Co., Savannah, Ga., 1862.

Elliott, Robert, and Elliott, Charlotte, grandchildren of the Rt. Rev. Stephen Elliott, who reside in Sewanee, Tenn. Personal interviews.

Fairbanks, G. R., *History of the University of the South*. H. and W. B. Drew Co., Jacksonville, Fla., 1905.

Guerry, Moultrie, *Men Who Made Sewanee*. University Press, Sewanee, Tenn., 1932.

Hanckel, Thomas M., editor, *Sermons by the Right Reverend Stephen Elliott, late Bishop of Georgia with a memoir by Thomas M. Hanckel*. Pott and Amory, New York, N. Y., 1867.

Hopkins, John Henry, Jr., *Life of the Late Rt. Rev. John Henry Hopkins*. F. J. Hemington & Co., New York, N. Y., 1873.

*Journals of the Diocese of Georgia*, 18th, 19th, 20th, 21st, 22nd, 23rd, 24th, 25th, 26th, 27th, 28th, 29th, 30th, 31st, 32nd, 33rd, 34th, 35th, 36th, 37th, 38th, 39th, Annual Conventions.

Lewis, David W., *Transactions of the Southern Central Agricultural Society, 1846-51*. Benjamin F. Griffin, Macon, Ga., 1852.

Pattee, Sarah Lewis, "Andrew Jackson Downing and His Influence on Landscape Architecture in America." In *Landscape Architecture Quarterly*. Vol. XIX, No. 2, p. 79.

Pennington, Edgar L., "Stephen Elliott, First Bishop of Georgia." In *Historical Magazine of the Protestant Episcopal Church*. Vol. VII, No. 3, p. 203.

White, George, *Statistics of the State of Georgia*. W. Thorne Williams, Savannah, Ga., 1849.

White, George, *Historical Collections of Georgia*. Pudney and Russell, New York, N. Y., 1854.

Wilmer, Richard Hooker, *In Memoriam. A Sermon in Commemoration of the Life and Labors of the Rt. Rev. Stephen Elliott (late Bishop of Georgia)*. Farrow and Dennett, Mobile, Ala., 1867.

www.ingramcontent.com/pod-product-compliance
Lightning Source LLC
Chambersburg PA
CBHW011721220426
43664CB00023B/2904